Epic Cars

Ford GT

JULIA GARSTECKI AND ANDREW DERKOVITZ

BLACK
RABBIT
BOOKS

Bolt is published by Black Rabbit Books
P.O. Box 3263, Mankato, Minnesota, 56002.
www.blackrabbitbooks.com
Copyright © 2020 Black Rabbit Books

Marysa Storm, editor; Catherine Cates,
interior designer; Grant Gould, cover designer;
Omay Ayres, photo researcher

Library of Congress Cataloging-in-Publication Data
Names: Garstecki, Julia, author. | Derkovitz, Andrew, author.
Title: Ford GT / by Julia Garstecki and Andrew Derkovitz.
Description: Mankato, Minnesota : Black Rabbit Books, [2020] | Series: Bolt.
Epic cars | Includes bibliographical references and index. | Audience: Ages 9-12. |
Audience: Grades 4 to 6.
Identifiers: LCCN 2018018003 (print) | LCCN 2018019260 (ebook) |
ISBN 9781680728453 (e-book) | ISBN 9781680728378 (library binding) |
ISBN 9781644660362 (paperback)
Subjects: LCSH: Ford GT automobile–Juvenile literature.
Classification: LCC TL215.F7 (ebook) | LCC TL215.F7 G37 2020 (print) |
DDC 629.222/2–dc23
LC record available at https://lccn.loc.gov/2018018003

Special thanks to Justin Storm for his help with this book.

Printed in the United States. 1/19

Contents

CHAPTER 1

Racing

Down the Road

With the push of a button,
the Ford GT roars to life. The driver
prepares for takeoff. She lowers
the car 2 inches (5 centimeters).
Its rear wing pops up. Then she hits
the gas pedal. The supercar screams.
With a flash, it races down the track.

COMPARING HORSEPOWER

2018
Ford
Mustan
Fastbac

460

Built to Race

In 1966, Ford's GT40 won a 24-hour race called Le Mans. In 2016, Ford won the race again with its redesigned GT. The new GT is a race car made for the street. Fans love its powerful look. But the car doesn't just look strong. With 647 **horsepower**, it leaves other cars in the dust.

2018 Dodge Challenger SRT 392	2018 Ford GT	2019 Chevrolet Corvette Z06
485	647	650

LARGE WINDSHIELD

HEADLIGHTS

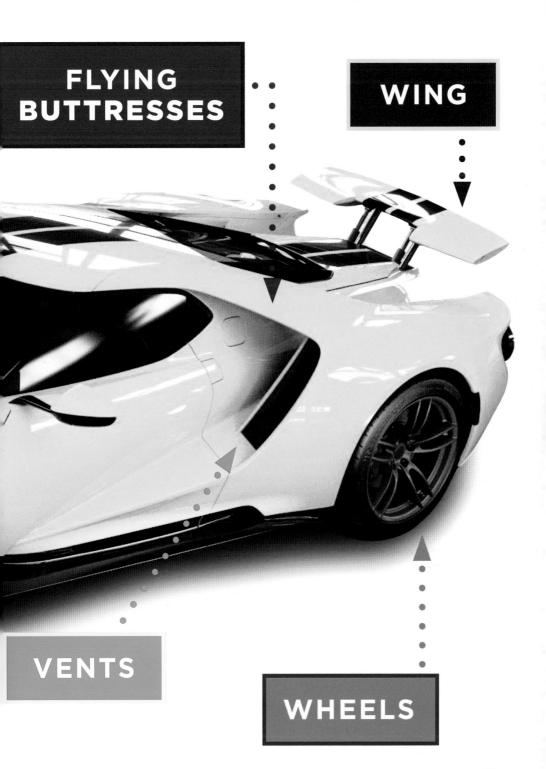

FLYING BUTTRESSES

WING

VENTS

WHEELS

9

The GT has an **aerodynamic** design. Its flying buttresses guide air over the car. By guiding air, the car increases **downforce**. It also cuts back on **drag**.

• •

Vents move fresh air to the engine. Hot air leaves through hollow taillights.

The GT has wide tires. Wider tires give a car more grip. More grip improves a car's handling.

A Wonderful Wing

The GT's wing has many purposes. It can rise up and tilt. Adjusting the wing increases downforce. The wing also acts as an air brake. It helps the car stop quickly.

Carbon Fiber

The GT has a carbon-fiber body.
Carbon fiber is strong. It makes a car
safe and sturdy. But the material is
also light. A lighter car is a faster car.
Carbon fiber is easier to shape than
other materials too. Cars made from
carbon fiber can have more curves.

The GT has
carbon fiber in the
interior too.

POWERED BY FORD

Options

Buyers have many ways to personalize their GTs. To begin, there are eight paint colors to choose from. There are seven different stripe options too. Lower parts of the car can have different **finishes**.

Buyers have many options when buying their GTs.

8
EXTERIOR COLORS

7
STRIPE OPTIONS

5
BRAKE CALIPER
COLORS

4
INTERIOR COLOR
COMBINATIONS

The GT doesn't
even come with
cup holders.

Inside

The GT's cabin is small. The driver and passenger sit close together. The interior is simple too. It's built so owners focus on driving. To save space, the seats don't move. Drivers adjust the steering wheels and gas pedals instead. Because of this design, the steering wheel has many controls.

CHAPTER 3

Power and Performance

The GT has a twin-turbo 3.5-liter V-6 engine. With it, the car rockets to 216 miles (348 kilometers) per hour. It flies from 0 to 60 miles (97 km) per hour in less than 3 seconds.

COMPARING TOP SPEEDS

2018 Aventador S

2018 Ford GT

2018 McLaren 720S

2018 812 Superfast

miles per hour

217 (349 km)

216 (348 km)

212 (341 km)

211 (340 km)

190   195   200   205   210   215   220

DRIVING MODES

WET MODE
best for
driving in rain

NORMAL MODE
best for
daily driving

SPORT MODE
best for
sporty driving

TRACK MODE
best for driving
on tracks

V-MAX MODE
best for fast
straight-line
driving

Driving Modes

The GT has five driving modes.
Drivers use Normal mode for
daily driving. The real excitement
happens in V-Max or Track
modes. In those modes, the car
lowers 2 inches (5 cm). Being
lower to the ground increases
stability. It makes the car more
aerodynamic too.

2
TOTAL SEATING

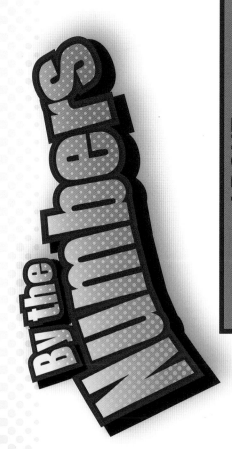

By the Numbers

ABOUT
$450,000
BASE PRICE

1,000

TOTAL NUMBER
OF GTS FORD
WILL SELL

about
18
miles (29 km)
per gallon

ESTIMATED
HIGHWAY MILEAGE

187.5
INCHES
(476 CM)
LENGTH

Few people can buy a GT. First, they must fill out a **questionnaire**. Then Ford decides if they can buy one.

CHAPTER 4

An Epic Car

The new GT amazes fans. It has incredible speed. And its design is unique. Fans can't wait to see what improvements come next.

aerodynamic (air-oh-dahy-NAM-ik)—something that is shaped so it moves easily through air

buttress (BUH-tris)—something that supports, props, or strengthens

caliper (KAL-uh-per)—a device used to press a brake pad against the sides of a brake rotor

downforce (doun-FAWRS)—a force that increases the stability of a motor vehicle by pressing it downward

drag (DRAYG)—something that makes action or progress slower or more difficult

finish (FIN-ish)—the final coating on a surface

horsepower (HORS-pow-uhr)—a unit used to measure the power of engines

mileage (MAHY-lij)—the average number of miles a vehicle will travel on a gallon of gasoline

questionnaire (kwes-chuh-NAIR)—a set of questions to be asked to a number of people, usually in order to gather information or opinions

stability (stuh-BIL-i-tee)—being able to remain steady and stable

BOOKS

Bodensteiner, Peter. *Supercars*. Gearhead Garage. Mankato, MN: Black Rabbit Books, 2017.

Fishman, Jon M. *Cool Sports Cars*. Awesome Rides. Minneapolis: Lerner Publications, 2019.

Machajewski, Sarah. *All about Cars*. Let's Find Out! Transportation. New York: Britannica Educational Publishing, 2017.

WEBSITES

Ford GT
www.caranddriver.com/ford/gt

Ford GT
www.fordgt.com/ph/performance/gt/

Ford GT Supercar
www.ford.com/performance/gt/

INDEX